T0195981

POWERFUL POTENTIAL OF PARENT(S):

*Critical Influences, Ages 0 to 5,
Extended into K-12 Grades*

AN ABRIDGED HANDBOOK

Dr. Donald R. Draayer, Educator
American Association of School Administrators (AASA)
NATIONAL SUPERINTENDENT OF YEAR

To order additional copies of this book, contact:
Xlibris
844-714-8691
www.Xlibris.com
Orders@Xlibris.com

ISBN: 978-1-6641-5262-5 (sc)
ISBN: 978-1-6641-5261-8 (e)

Print information available on the last page

Rev. date: 01/15/2021

PREFACE

What is the job of a parent?

To love a new human being and

to prepare him/her for life's challenges.

This responsibility begins with the **start of pregnancy** when a male sperm unites with a female egg and starts a human life.

> The parent's role continues for one's lifetime; however, *the nine months of pregnancy and first eighteen years of life* **are most influential!**

> In this timeframe, the complete **dependency** of the fetus and newborn must be turned into **independency** of the youth – *and readiness to function and contribute positively within the adult world.*

A parent's love is not an <u>abstract notion</u>.

> It is a daily and nightly duty of nourishing, caring, protecting, teaching, and guiding a new human through stages of physical, mental, and emotional growth, discovering purpose, surprise, and joy of the next generation coming into its own, and leaving behind a true measure of our gift to humanity.

Thousands of books, advice columns in magazines, lectures in vast auditoriums, and expansive electronic media give advice on *wise parenting practices*.

<u>This</u> **ABRIDGED HANDBOOK** <u>cuts to the heart of the subject for new and busy parents.</u> It is NOT about *blaming* or *shaming* anyone; rather, its purpose is to inform and focus on what needs to be done so **all children 0 to 18** can learn, love, and strive academically, socially, and become ready for adult responsibilities. **When even one youth is "left behind" in life's journey, *<u>the whole of humanity suffers</u>*.**

DEDICATION

To all parent(s)
who have daily contact, responsibility, and deep desire to promote
the potential *in the lives of their children, ages 0 to 18.*

To all who serve parent(s)
and their preschool children in well-baby health clinic visits, childcare
facilities, preschool nurseries, and through supportive nonprofit
organizations – all of whom are partners in early childhood education.

To all who teach K-12 children and youth
so that *academics* are learned, *social skills* are instilled, and a deep *sense
of caring* is implanted toward other human beings in a world
where interdependency is an imperative for all aspects of living.

To all public officials
who make laws and rules that impact the welfare of *all children,*
provide funding for their care and instruction, and exercise
oversight of service deliveries on the frontlines.

TABLE OF CONTENTS

CHAPTER 1

WHAT "RESEARCH" TELLS US ABOUT PREGNANCY

A *new life* starts the *very moment* the female egg and male sperm unite in conception. A new human cell (zygote) is formed; it undergoes thousands of cell divisions over the next nine months. Within four weeks, head, eyes, heart, and buds for arms and legs are visible.

A pregnant woman is the solo hostess to the fetus *every minute of every day and night*. Consciously and unconsciously, the mother is the source of **physical** and **emotional** sustenance to the fetus. Both have carry-over influence into childhood and beyond.

The pictures below show two fetus brains, one normal, and the other subjected to Fetal Alcohol Syndrome, which demonstrates the *stunting* of brain development due to alcohol consumption. Drug use likewise impacts *mother and fetus*; they share the same intake.

HEALTHY, NORMAL FETAL BRAIN

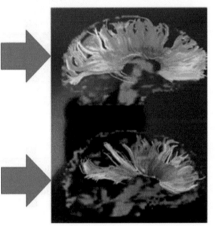

**ABNORMAL FETAL BRAIN
DUE TO ALCOHOL USE (Fetal
Alcohol Syndrome)**

Even one drink during pregnancy can impact the fetus brain development, and *alcoholism or drug use* of the mother can severely disable fetus learning and functioning for the whole of its eventual lifetime outside the womb. (Note: Up to one-third of women are *unaware* they are pregnant until the third month of a nine-month pregnancy.)

Moreover, severe nutritional shortages for pregnant mothers can harm fetal bodily development, too, as witnessed in children born to mothers living amid sustained drought or severe poverty. Furthermore, the brain of the fetus hears external sounds while in the womb. Discordant sounds such as *angry voices* close at hand are upsetting and are compounded in their effect when accompanied by *physical altercations*.

> These linkages between the well-being of the pregnant mother and the unborn fetus are absolute. Critical linkages continue after birth!

CHAPTER 2

THE NEW BORN'S FIRST CRY: *HELP ME! LOVE ME!*

Birth brings shocking change for the fetus. Passage through the tight birth canal traumatizes the mother and baby. The fluid-filled, even-temperature womb is now history; outside air now envelopes the baby's whole body, causing a burst of tears and a crying out, which clears the passageway for fresh air (oxygen) to enter the baby's lungs.

This scene plays itself out in every human birth throughout the world, regardless skin color, birth country, religion, parental education, wealth, or forebearer history. The umbilical cord to the mother is cut; nourishment, henceforth comes from external sources.

From this point forward the baby's *environment* plays a much larger role than most of us imagine. Instinctively, the baby cuddles against mother's warm body; the mouth seeks the source of milk nourishment and soon is satisfied. Eyes close and the body falls to sleep to revitalize energy -- a life rhythm to be repeated at all hours of the day and night!

Noteworthy, the new baby will recognize his or her mother voice, because *while in uterus,* the brain hears and remembers that voice which enhances the bonding process outside the womb. At birth, all human senses of the newborn, such as sight, touch, taste, smell, and hearing are ready to take in its new surroundings.

Who engages with the infant? Mother, father, or both? Are there siblings? Are there other family members or friends who seek to touch, hold, speak, and relate to this baby? Sorting out differences among people comes early as the baby's brain records differences in (word) sounds, interprets facial expressions, and *puts them into memory automatically.* This is nature's order and gift to human development.

Adults often underestimate the speed of the baby's brain growth through the rapid subdivision of its cells and **how significant** are the cognitive and early social-emotional foundations that are being recorded within the brain.

> A raft of cultural influences impact all human experiences; they are
> at work during the whole of life, but none more so than in the
> first five years of life.
> READ ON…

KEY ELEMENTS FOR EARLY SUCCESS

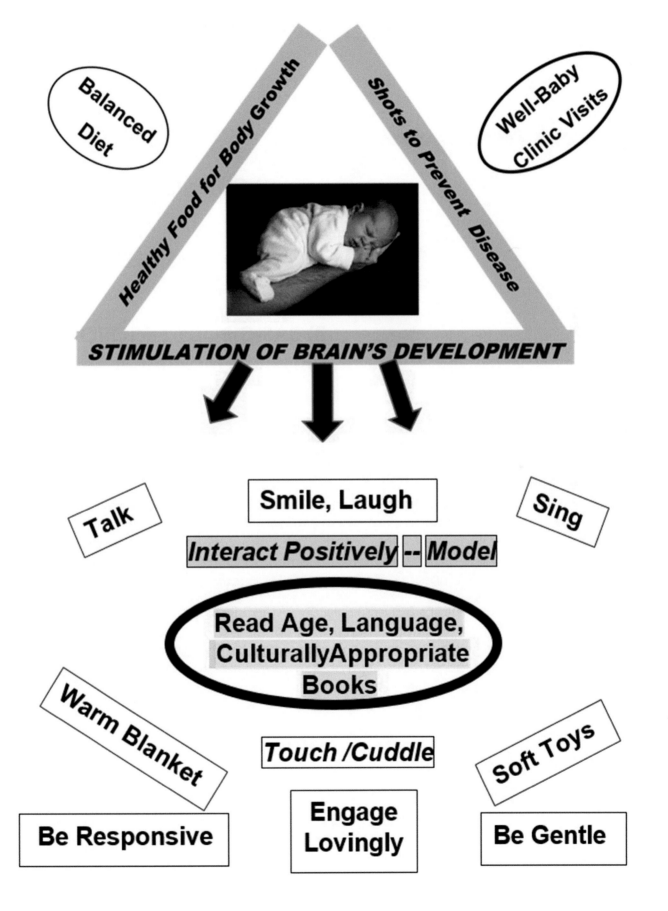

Balanced Diet

Healthy Food for Body Growth

Shots to Prevent Disease

Well-Baby Clinic Visits

STIMULATION OF BRAIN'S DEVELOPMENT

Talk

Smile, Laugh

Sing

Interact Positively -- Model

Read Age, Language, CulturallyAppropriate Books

Warm Blanket

Touch /Cuddle

Soft Toys

Be Responsive

Engage Lovingly

Be Gentle

CHAPTER 3

THREE BRAIN FUNCTIONS THROUGHOUT LIFE

The human brain is wonderfully formed with cellular growth progression at different speeds and times of life. <u>The first five years of life are *foundational* and *most impactful!*</u>

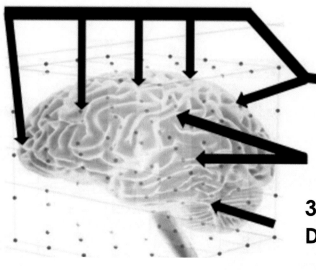

1) COGNITION -- *THINKING*

2) EMOTIONS -- FEELINGS

3) BASIC BODY FUNCTIONS -- Digestion, Movement, Blinking

1. **Basic body functions** – e.g., breathing, movement, seeing, hearing, sucking, swallowing, vocal sounds (e.g., crying), digestion, and bowel movement -- are normally operant at birth. The control center of many basic body functions is located at the base of the brain, around the top of the spinal cord.

2. **Early** (*social-emotional*) **feelings** *within* the fetus are generated and recorded within the brain and are *greatly ramped up* (after birth and first five years of life) by interactions with the world outside the mother womb. These *early feelings* serve as a baseline for the infant and child -- put in the brain's basement so to speak -- *which then become a reference point when subsequent life experiences occur.*

    New social situations are immediately judged (consciously or unconsciously) *in accord with past social experiences;* the specifics of past experiences may or may not be remembered, but they do play an **active behavioral role in present situations**, including fear, anger, fight, flight or (conversely) reciprocating smiles, outreaching arms, willingness to be held, forming of new friendships, and determination to accomplish goals, rather than giving up.

3. **THINKING** (cognitive-thought ability) ALSO tracks *very strongly* with <u>early childhood brain growth</u> and <u>life's developmental experiences</u>.

    A child's cognitive brain cells are connected by exposure to sounds, pictures, touch, and taste. Much repetition strengthens these connections, enhancing memory and clarity of understanding of letters, words, and their meaning. The final brain cell growth (late teens/early 20s) occurs in the frontal lobe of the brain (above the eyes) which controls executive function skills.

CHAPTER 4

CRITICAL IMPACT: PRE-SCHOOL BRAIN DEVELOPMENT

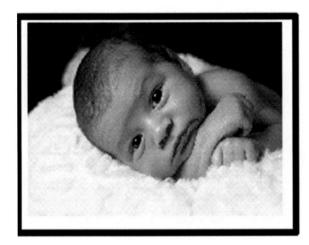 

Time-lapse-infrared photos show that more new brain cells are **formed in the *first year (and years)* of life than in all later years in life. *Parent(s)/caregiver(s) are enablers of that brain's development.***

At birth, a baby's brain is about one third the size of an adult's brain. In 90 days, it more than doubles its volume, to 55% of its final size. By age two the *infant 's physical* brain size is roughly the *same size as an adult*, but what cannot be seen by the naked eye is the ***growth of new cells*** inside the brain, which comes about by means of ***extraordinarily rapid cell division.***

Indeed, at this point in life nearly twice as many cells are being formed than will survive early childhood! **Synapses (connective links) must form among these cells for them to function and be retained.** A great many of these unconnected cells die (sluff off), disappear, and do not regenerate later.

At birth unfocused eyes will soon differentiate among faces, follow movement, and direct body movement. The inability of a baby at birth to hold up its head or move at will changes over time to turning its head, rolling over, then crawling, and often walking by the year's end. Parent(s) are amazed/stunned by the *visible* daily progress.

Thus, *external environment stimulations* provided by the parent(s)/caregivers in the first years of a child's life *are critical*; they determine what cells become connected *and are retained* for lifelong use – feeling, thinking, memory -- that are so essential for social interaction, lifelong learning, and judgment.

CHAPTER 5

THE INFANT'S RAPID GROWTH IS ASTOUNDING

The human body grows *more rapidly* in **the first year of life** outside the womb
than any later time frame in life.

Data below:
Help Me Grow
Minnesota Dept.
of Education

Your Baby at 3 Months
- Follows movement by turning head
- Lifts head and chest when lying on stomach
- Moves arms and legs easily
- Startles at loud noises
- Cries, smiles, coos
- Quiets to family voice or touch

Family/Caregiver Role at 3 Months
- Provide interesting things to look at
- Talk, sing, and read to baby
- Put baby to sleep on their back
- Cuddle baby and touch baby gently
- Respond to baby's cries and coos
- Hold baby when feeding

Your Baby at 6 Months
- Rolls over in both directions
- Begins to sit with a little help
- Coos, babbles, squeals, laughs
- Knows familiar faces and begins to know if someone is a stranger
- Uses hands and mouth to explore the world
- Transfers objects from hand to hand

Family/Caregiver Role at 6 Months
- Look at and read books with baby
- Introduce liquids in a cup
- Talk to and play with baby
- Be predictable and consistent with baby
- Watch and learn what baby wants/needs
- Place toys near so baby can move and reach for them

Your Baby at 9 Months
- Sits well without support
- Creeps or crawls
- Holds 2 objects at the same time
- Responds to own name
- Makes sounds like "dada" "mama", "baba"
- Shows feelings by smiling, crying, pointing

Family/Caregiver Role at 9 Months
- Play games, sing songs, and say rhymes
- Be available, responsive, and gentle
- Talk to baby about what you and baby are seeing or doing
- Give baby safe place to move around
- Read books with baby
- Name feelings like happy, mad, sad

Your Toddler at 12 Months
- Pulls to stand, walks holding unto furniture
- Uses simple gestures, like shaking head "no" or waving bye-bye
- Says "mama" and "dada"
- Shows preferences for certain people/toys
- Imitates gestures, sounds, and actions
- Puts objects in and out of containers

Family/Caregiver Role at 12 Months
- Include toddler at family meals
- Play, read, sing, and talk to toddler
- Let toddler turn pages when looking at book together
- Help toddler learn limits by saying "no" in a firm quiet voice and by providing choices
- Use words to tell toddler "what comes next"
- Develop and maintain consistent routines

CHAPTER 6

DEVEOPMENTAL LADDER FROM 18 MONTHS TO YEAR 3

The progression of a **toddler's learning** is *unrelenting*
when well encouraged by family and other caregivers.

(SOURCE: **Help Me Grow**, Minnesota Department of Education)

At 18 Months, Your Toddler
- Walks alone; begins to run
- Says three or more words
- Tries new things with familiar adults nearby
- Points to one body part
- Scribbles with a crayon or pencil
- Shows interests in other children

Family/Caregiver Role at 18 Months
- Provide toys without or minus small pieces
- Hold toddler and read simple stories
- Set limits that are firm, fair, and consistent
- Encourage curiosity
- Play games and sing songs with movements that toddler can imitate

---

At 2 Years, Your Toddler
- Kicks a ball forward
- Walks up and down stairs holding on
- Points to things and pictures in a book when named
- Uses 2 or 3 words together
- Plays briefly beside other children
- Builds towers of 4 or more blocks

Family/Caregiver Role at 2 Years
- Talk to toddler about things you and they are doing and seeing
- Be calm and comforting after temper outbursts. Be consistent with what toddler can and cannot do
- Talk to toddler and use words for feelings
- Encourage and praise toddler
- Tell stories, read, and encourage pretend play

At 3 Years, Your Child
- Climbs and runs well
- Builds with blocks; a tower of 6 blocks
- Uses 3-word sentences
- Shows concern and affection for others
- Plays make-believe with dolls, animals & people
- Does puzzles with 3 to 4 pieces

Family/Caregiver Role at 3 Years
- Let child help with simple household chores
- Help child include others in play, taking turns
- Support child to develop trust in other consistent adults
- Listen to and encourage child to use many words and longer sentences
- Share new stories, songs, games, and play materials
- Support appropriate expression of feelings

Portion of Toddler BRAIN that is fully engaged by AGE THREE

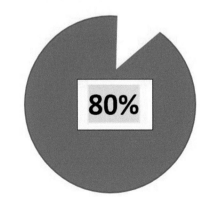

80%

CHAPTER 7

DEVEOPMENTAL LADDER FROM 4 TO 5 YEARS

The progression of a child's **brain-power-learning** and what a family/caregiver can do to best prepare him or her for kindergarten readiness, K-12 education, and life thereafter is shown below. (SOURCE: **Help Me Grow**, Minnesota Department of Education)

At 4 Years, Your Child
- Catches a bounced ball most of the time
- Tells stories and recalls parts of stories
- Plays cooperatively with other children
- Copies simple shapes
- Understands the concept of "same" and "different"
- Follows instructions with 2 or 3 steps

Family/Caregiver Role at 4 Years
- Give child crayons, markers and a variety of play materials
- Read with child every day
- Pay attention when child is talking
- Give child opportunities to play with other children
- Say positive things to child
- Urge child to use words to ask for help

At 5 Years, Your Child
- Hops; may be able to skip
- Speaks clearly in sentences of 5 or more words
- Counts 10 or more objects
- Draws a person with at least 6 body parts
- Wants to please friends & wants to be like friends

Family/Caregiver Role at 5 Years
- Read, Read, Read to child
- Catch child being good and encourage all the things they do
- Point out familiar symbols and words for the child to know
- Gently and consistently help child manage feelings and control behavior
- Be patient and responsive to questions
- Provide opportunities for physical play

Portion of Child BRAIN that is fully engaged by AGE FIVE

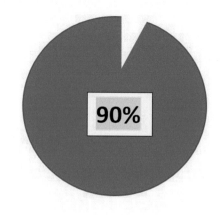

90%

CHAPTER 8

"SCHOOLING" STARTS AT BIRTH, *NOT KINDERGARTEN*

Scientific brain research shows that the *family and neighborhood* make huge impacts on a child's brain development, **ages 0 to 5.** Environmental factors in these settings determine *cognitive and social-emotional preparedness for learning during K-12 school years.* All children learn in K-12, **but the speed and depth of learning in K-12 *can vary widely.***

> Children who are well prepared *cognitively and socially* for K-12 classroom school instruction **not only learn, *but soar*,** whereas other children *are also learning but at slower paces.*

> This can largely be attributed to differences in child raising practices in their homes/neighborhoods, especially ages 0 to 5, which impacts brain development and *has direct influence* in two relevant areas: 1) *cognitive (thinking) ability and 2) social behavior norms within school and neighborhood settings.*

From elementary school through high school, the (2002) *Federal No Child Left Behind Act* has required achievement testing. Also, the law requires the reporting of results for individual school buildings and racial sub-groups. This wide-spread testing and reporting began in the 1970's as part of the "**school accountability movement**" across America.

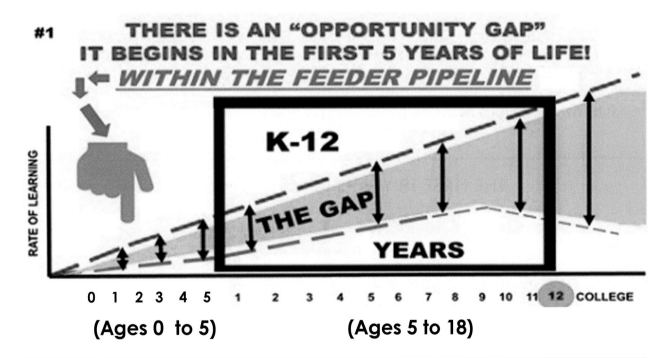

Home/neighborhood factors explaining "the gaps" during 0 to 5 years *tend to persist in K-12 years. Most "gap" pupils show progress in K-12, but full "catch-up stories" are relatively rare, and school dropout-statistics are shocking.*

CHAPTER 9

CHILD'S *"AWAKE TIME"* in HOME/NEIGHBORHOODS *FAR EXCEEDS* HOURS IN K-12 SCHOOL SETTINGS

Ages 0-1 & 1-2: **Sleep 12 hours/Awake 12 hours**
12 awake hours x 365 days x 2 years = **8,760 hours**
Awake hours all spent in home/neighborhood settings; zero in K-12 Schools

Ages 2-3, 3-4, & 4-5: **Sleep 10 hours/Awake 14 hours**
14 awake hours x 365 days x 3 years = **15,330 hours**
All hours all spent at home or in neighborhood settings; zero in K-12 Schools

Ages 5-6, 6-7, 7-8, 8-9, 9-10, & 10-11: **Sleep 9 hours/Awake 15 hours**
15 hours awake x 365 days x 6 years = **32,850** awake hours divided as follows:
K-5 Elementary School: (6.5 hours, including lunch) x 170 days x 6 years = **6,630 hours**
Home/neighborhood time: 8.5 hours x 170 school days x 6 years = **8,670 hours***
*Assumes students walk or ride buses to school with local neighborhood kids.
Plus, remaining home/neighborhood time: 15 hours x 195 days x 6 years = **17,550 hours**
Sum: awake in home/neighborhood (26,200) vs. K-5 school (6630) (ratio: 3.95 to 1)

Ages 11-18, Public Secondary Level, Grades 6-12: **Sleep 8 hrs./Awake 16 hrs.**
x 365 days per year x 7 years = **40,880** awake hrs. divided as follows:
3 Middle + 4 High School Years = 6.5 hrs.(including lunch) x 170 days x 7 yrs. = **7,735 hrs.**
Plus 2.0 hrs. per school day for extracurriculars = 2.0 x 170 days x 7 years = **2,380 hrs.***
Assumes students walk or ride buses to school with local neighborhood kids so home/neighborhood time on schools' days: 7.5 hrs.. x 170 days x 7 years = **8,925 hrs.*
Sum: awake hours in home/neighborhood (30,765) vs. publicly funded 6-12 (10,118)
(ratio: 3.04 to 1)

THE FIRST 18 YEARS OF A YOUTH'S LIFE

IN HOME/NEIGHBORHOODS	IN PUBLIC FUNDED SCHOOLS
8,760 hrs. -- age 0 – 2	0,000 hrs. -- age 0 - 2
15,330 hrs. -- age 2 – 5	0,000 hrs. -- age 2 - 5
26,200 hrs. -- grades K-5	6,630 hrs. – grades K - 5
30,765 hrs. -- grades 6 - 12	10,118 hrs. – grades 6 - 12
81,055 hrs. -- 0 - 18	16,748 hrs. – 0 - 18

OVERALL RATIO – 4.84 to 1.0 – AGES 0 to 18

CHAPTER 10

ADVERSE CHILDHOOD EXPERIENCES

Past chapters shared what parents of 0 to 5 children **can do _to advance_** their start in life. Here are **ACES (Adverse Childhood Experiences)** _to be avoided, stopped_!

In the 1980s pediatricians in Boston, Massachusetts, who served parents and children throughout this large metropolitan city, conferred together about why some children were thriving and other struggling. Their concerted study identified factors that harm, damage, destroy environments in homes in which children are raised. Their list morphed over intervening years by other studies throughout the USA, giving rise to this list: **_Adverse Childhood Experiences_**

READING ALOUD IS DOCTOR-RECOMMENDED

ABUSE

Physical
Sexual
Emotional/Verbal

NEGLECT

Emotional
Verbal

HOUSEHOLD DYSFUNCTION

Mental Illness
Domestic Violence
Divorce/Separation
Incarceration
Alcohol/Drugs/Abuse

ADVERSE CHILDHOOD EXPERIENCES
They are found in all sectors of American society but more so in homes and neighborhoods where socio-economic factors (_especially poverty_) play a heavy role. When three of more on this list are in a child's life, rarely does the pupil graduate from high school.

Families by their circumstances live in housing areas where **_their income_** can pay the rent or mortgage; families in poverty have fewer locational choices and are typically congregated in separate sections of a village, town, or city. Domestic and neighborhood problems are more commonplace in these settings, and children in the poverty zones experience more _opportunity gaps_ that are reflected in their academic performance and social relationships when they enter kindergarten.

CHAPTER 11

GOOD PARENTING -- A TEAM ENDEAVOR

Research shows a child -- who grows up with *at least* one adult who is consistently present, actively engaged, and a positive influence -- will better travel life's rough roads, but *a larger supportive team* <u>greatly improves</u> the odds!

We humans are social beings; we engage, learn from one another, make judgements, and must reach out for help in the raising of an infant, child, and youth.

A significant "other" loving relationship (husband, wife, partner) heads the list; two can confer and share in the daily decision-making and follow-through engagement with the child; it doubles and reinforces what the offspring touches, hears, sees, and uses as a frame of reference while growing up.

A well-rounded support team includes <u>parent(s)</u>, <u>siblings</u>, <u>uncles</u>, <u>aunts</u>, <u>grandparents</u>, <u>friends</u>, <u>neighbors</u>, and <u>community members at-large</u>. **Altogether,** this team of caregivers provides the cognitive and social environment for the baby, infant, child, and youth. When societal benefits go more to some youth than others, for whatever reason, the shortfall diminishes the whole and the parts.

Unfortunately, child predators are in all sectors of society. Most *often they are discovered within a child's inner, trusted circle (the enlarged family)*, and sometimes in institutions or organizations providing services to children.

<u>Being on guard is *everyone's* business</u>, *especially the child's parent(s).*
Frequent moves of the parent(s) and child to new living quarters or the placement of the child into different domestic settings *fractionalizes* social networks; it undermines in variable degrees the inner security and knowledge a child should be developing for eventual adulthood, and it can foster repeats in generational patterns.

CHAPTER 12

K-5 GRADES – LETTING GO -- YET STAY CONNECTED

The expression, "starting school", is a misnomer because the first 5 years of childhood are filled with academic learning and socialization which are *fully home guided and directed*. Now, at age 5, *institutionalized learning and socialization* are required by law, which commonly **engenders two conflicting emotional responses** in parent(s):

> ***Relief:*** *"Someone else (teachers in a formalized school setting) will be responsible for my child at least for 6 ½ hours a day for 170 days a year. Public taxes pay nearly 100% of the cost."*
>
> ***Anxiety:*** *" How well will my child adjust to new surroundings and what roles can I play at home and school to make school learning a positive experience?"*

Enrollment in elementary school, grades K-5, constitutes the *first 6 years* of a 13-year *home/school/child partnership*. There is steady growth in cognitive thought (reading, writing, and math), content is remembered, curiosity grows, and speed of movement accelerates. ***Children sense when home and school are working together on their behalf.***

K-5 RECOMMENDATIONS

- **Learn the territory!** Attend school-sponsored events to meet the teacher, see your student's classroom, and meet and mix with others on this educational journey.
- **Stay abreast of student homework.** Read everything the school sends home with your student. Be informed so you can discuss and reinforce your child's learning.
- **Attend parent/teacher conferences.** They are set up for the parent(s) to hear about the student's progress, ask questions, and also *provide parent perspectives to the teacher.*,
- **Contact the teacher** if you have upsetting changes in your homelife, have concerns about your child's progress, or you feel uneasy about "school stories" he or she brings home.
- **Establish consistent home routines.** Like good nutrition and sleep hours, as well as time for homework, play, and *READING*. Also, especially important, **monitor interactions with the child's siblings and friends.** Remain breast of and guide positive relationships.

CHAPTER 13

LIFE'S CHALLENGES IN GRADES 6 to 8 -- A "WILD RIDE"

These are adolescent growth years in grades 6, 7, and 8 (middle school), followed by four "teen years" in grades 9, 10, 11, and 12 (high school). Pupils in middle school can read, write, compute, use technology, and learn independently and in groups. Their bodies change rapidly toward the end of this age span. They shoot upward -- girls first, boys close behind. Males win this height race.

Hormones surge, mood swings occur. Emotions are on a kind of roller coaster with periodic swing shifts directed inwardly and outwardly. Friendship groups expand, contract, shift, and reform periodically. Name calling is commonplace. Anger mounts; forgiveness less so.

Deeper life questions begin to occupy their inner thoughts. Cultural identity is explored. Where do I fit within the human race? What is my genetic background and with whom do I want to be identified? The wish is to belong to something *bigger than self alone*. Gang recruitment by older students can be tempting for some, and interest/participation in school sports and extra-curricular activities grows.

Parent(s) ask, where did my "little" boy or girl go? Who is this stranger in my house? The adolescent wants independence, but still lacks mature judgment. Argumentation is commonplace. Of note, many teachers decline assignments with middle school year students; still others seek, relish, and enjoy the challenges of adolescence. (*Parents do not have that choice.*)

RECOMMENDATIONS, Grades 6, 7, 8

- **Read a good book on adolescence at end of the 6th grade.** Parent(s) and son/daughter read it; then discuss it together. Pinpoint predictable behaviors; record them; **all <u>sign</u> a record for future reference.**
- **In the heat of later turmoil(s), call a family conference, reread the signed record sheet.** Remind *each other that none of us is going crazy. This* is difficult passage time in life. Someone say, "*Hard as this time is, we love each other. Together, we can and will get through this life's phase.*"
- **If not started earlier, institute a saving account** for possible college attendance.
- ***Praise high effort and achievement*** of son or daughter, noting it opens future life options.
- **Be clear about should *NOT BE* put into e-mails and the internet and WHY.**
- **Continue recommendations for K-5 years (previous page); they still apply in middle school.**

CHAPTER 14

HIGH SCHOOL -- BRAIN & BODY BOTH ADDRESS OPTIONS

These four years imply *progression* by the very names given to each grade level: <u>freshmen</u>; <u>sophomore</u>, <u>junior,</u> and <u>senior</u>. These are the last years in public school with full taxpayer support -- a capstone time and launching pad into major life choices.

A student's body grows to adult height and adult-like strength. The brain becomes fully formed, except for a portion of the frontal lobe that controls "executive functioning" which completes its physical growth journey in late teens to early 20's. The curriculum includes required courses and a variety of optional courses. Co-curricular options typically include sports, arts, drama, and speech.

The sex drive functions also -- who to date and what personal boundary lines to follow. Money issues arise again and again -- clothes, entertainment, transportation needs, and what post-secondary options can be afforded. Should a part-time job be secured? How much to spend and save? What are the teen's curfews? Expect strong differences of opinion! All parties will need to work out solutions/compromises patiently -- *and not forget to reaffirm love for one another in the family setting.*

Parenting through the high school years shifts from *sole-to-joint* decision-making which brings family history and personalities of all parties into full play, as well as heightened tension, and need for problem solving skills. Dependent and independent role relationships are reconfigured almost daily and sometimes require consultative help -- relatives, friends, school guidance counselors, social workers, and experts in money management.

RECOMMENDATIONS, Grades 9, 10, 11, 12
- **Kiss the joy as it flies** – accept life's changes, mellow-out; be more a companion -- less the boss.
- **Talk to families who had or yet have high school students –** commiserate, celebrate, cry if it helps.
- **Formally schedule family counsel times into your busy lives –** to share, stay in touch, listen, learn.
- **Attend school functions** (plays, games, concerts, parent/teacher conferences) -- show interest/care.
- **Be actively available to the emerging adult –** job applications, visiting colleges, balancing priorities.
- **Jointly discuss** course selections, academic progress, post H.S. options, *and* budget realities.
- **Remember bluster and bombast** often are covering doubt and insecurity; <u>do not retaliate in kind</u>.
- **Forgive mistakes,** give encouragement in the rebounds, and express pride in progress.

CHAPTER 15

MAJOR THEMES FROM THIS ABRIDGED HANDBOOK

This Abridged HANDBOOK on a child's brain development draws upon scientific research and practical experience; it connects home and neighborhood with K-12 schools (and society at large) as **essential partners**.

MAJOR THEMES

1. The future of a human life begins at conception and is shaped by life experiences in the womb which have significant, lifelong impact. *Alcohol and drugs are dangerous threats to the fetus!*

2. **"Schooling"** begins not in K-12 but <u>the first 5 years in the home/neighborhood</u>. The baby/infant/child's brain cells connect to each other when stimulated by environmental interactions. Unconnected brain cells die or remain forever dormant, if not stimulated, in these early years. ***Singing, talking, READING, playing, are positive interactions.***

3. **ADVERSE CHILDHOOD EXPERIENCES** (ACES) – abuse, neglect, household dysfunction – ***play havoc with normal brain development for all youth, 0 - 18.***

4. Children at age 5 are enrolled in kindergarten. Some or many come with "opportunity gaps" from their home/neighborhood environment; they <u>all learn</u> but *not at the same speed or depth* as those with fewer (or no) opportunity gaps in their preschool years.

5. Those "opportunity gaps" manifest themselves in two arenas: 1) *cognitive thinking* [e.g., knowing words and their meanings] and/or 2) *social/emotional behavior* [e.g., getting along in larger group learning situations].

6. This early "opportunity gap" soon reveals itself during K-12 years in social behavior and/or lower achievement (standardized testing) and is commonly titled "school achievement gap" – often by public school critics.

    a. Much public perception is that K-12 schools can (or should be able to) *"reduce/end"* the achievement gap. Millions and billions of dollars have been spent to this end over many years in K-12 with limited success. Why?

    b. All classroom children *do learn*, including those with early "opportunity gaps" in their history. But those who have <u>few or no early childhood gaps</u> *learn faster (and soar)*, thus widening the margin of "the achievement gap" over the span of K-12 years.

7. Research and K-12 school testing now reveal that "achievement gaps" are closely aligned with social-economics of parent(s) and that <u>family poverty is the most pervasive factor</u>. *It is not that parents in poverty do not love their children.* **They do!** What is missing is the "means" -- time, money, and/or "know-how" -- to enrich their home/neighborhood environment and to work together with schools, which families with higher incomes do.

CHAPTER 16

MAKING PRESCHOOL EDUCATION AFFORDABLE TO FAMILIES IN POVERTY – OUR TWENTY-FIRST CENTURY CHALLENGE

Study after study conclude that family income is highly correlated with school achievement. Also, "opportunity gaps" among children are most commonplace among families in poverty. Who are these families? Cited below are two of many examples:

> Many American families in poverty have lived in USA for generations, wherein racial history, family dysfunction, and loss of hope roadblocks their upward mobility. When rent is due and is not paid, there are frequent moves to other living quarters. Frustrations mount, emotions rise, anger shows its ugly head, and divorce or abandonment results in more solo parenting and/or many short-time hook-ups, and multiple children. This modeling by the adult(s) seems "normal" to the children, which is then copied/repeated in their adult life. Tough cycle to end – our society's 21ˢᵗ Century CHALLENGE!

> Many and perhaps most immigrant families who arrive in the USA have limited knowledge of English, are hard workers, and use all their income for shelter, food, clothing, health care, and job transportation, e.g., distant walking, bicycle, bus, train, or car. They work full-time, plus a part-time job, or hold two or three part-time jobs. This limits contact time with their own children. *Also, their budget limitations can rarely cover tuition costs for day-care services or a preschool nursery program, family vacations, trips to the zoo, arboretum, etc.*

Currently, Minnesota (tax) support for daycare and preschool education barely scratches the surface of need, *especially for families in poverty*. What small amount is available is income-based and directed to preschool programs.

One small, new step taken by the MN Legislature was a $75,000 appropriation during 2020 and 2021 to **Reach Out And Read MN (ROR)**. This nonprofit works with Heath Clinic pediatricians across the state to add a third message in well-baby clinic visits: 1) shots for disease; 2) healthy food for body growth, and 3) **READ** *age, language, and culturally appropriate books to pre-school children to stimulate brain growth and cognitive development.* One such book to this end is given at the end of every doctor visit.

Expansion of pre-school services, especially to families in poverty, deserves and requires more state support. This is a political/financial challenge with these paybacks: **1)** decrease in opportunity gaps among children living in poverty; **2)** future reduction in "K-12 achievement gaps and drop-outs"; and **3)** a wise -- long-term investment -- in our economy, citizenry, and social order. Clearly this pathway works for families with means.

SOME MINNESOTA NON-PROFIT ORGANIZATIONS SUPPORTING OUR LITTLEST ONES

Little Moments Count: https://www.littlemomentscount.org "This is a statewide movement to help parents and the community understand the importance of talking, playing, reading, and singing early and often with children. We are a collaborative of organizations working to help increase parent and community interaction with babies and children. Provides a wealth of tools, services and advocacy for mothers, fathers, grandparents, caregivers, and extended families and for professionals."

Think Small: Parent Powered Texts info@thinksmall.org "Mission: To advance quality care and education of children in their crucial early years. Think Small will advance and develop innovative ideas that allow us to educate, engage and empower parents and caregivers so they have the information and resources they need to prepare their children for kindergarten." To these ends, parents can sign up for *weekly electronic text messages*, **at no charge**, that succinctly give reminders of parent-based activities pertinent to the age of their pre-school children.

Reach Out and Read MN https://reachoutandreadmn.org "We work with doctors and nurses to bring the brain-building power of books and reading into young children's regular pediatric care. We currently serve over 180,000 children and their families across Minnesota, providing them with developmentally and culturally appropriate books and coaching them on how to best aid in their child's early development."

Way to Grow https://www.givemn.org/organization/Waytogrow "Way to Grow is an early childhood and elementary education nonprofit that provides critical, holistic school-readiness and home visiting services to some of the most isolated families in Minneapolis, Brooklyn Park, and Brooklyn Center. Supporting families with children from birth to age eight, we work every day to empower our next generation of leaders."

The Family Partnership https://www.thefamilypartnership.org "Our nationally accredited (National Association for the Education of Young Children) and <u>Parent Aware</u> 4-Star multicultural therapeutic preschools prepare children for Kindergarten success and beyond. We offer developmental screenings on-site and provide speech, occupational, physical, music and play therapy to enhance learning potential. We help kids reach their goals and provide home visits to help parents resolve issues and support their children's success in school. Our staff also provides coaching and tutoring for older children and teens.

Public School Community Services (Early Childhood/Family Education) In 1972, the Minnesota Legislature authorized local school districts to offer community services before and beyond K-12 and provided a small (optional local tax levy) to help with funding, the balance of which comes from user-paid tuition for services received. Early Childhood/Family Education Classes are offered in many school districts, many using a sliding scale for tuition fees based upon family income.

The above organizations are but a few of the entities in Minnesota that advocate for -- and provide services to -- parents of pre-school children, and older youth, too. Day Care facilities and Classes for Pre-K pupils abound <u>but most service providers must charge service fees that are prohibitive to families living in poverty.</u> These inequities in parental "means" underscore the presence of pre-school "opportunity gaps" ages 0-5 and "achievement gaps" K-12 -- and a starting point for society's care for <u>all its littlest ones</u>.

RECORD OF BOOKS READ BY PARENT(S) DURING THESE STAGES: BABY/INFANT/TODDLER

	Hash Marks For # Times Read

RECORD OF BOOKS PRE-KINDERGARTENER LOVES TO READ WITH ADULT HELP OR BY HIMSELF/HERSELF

Hash Marks For # Times Read

RESUME
Donald (Don) Draayer Ed. D.

BIRTH/UPBRINGING:
- Born in Albert Lea, MN on 11-8-1935 to second generation immigrants from Holland
- Oldest of four siblings on a small truck farm in Hollandale, MN

EDUCATION:
- High School Diploma, Albert Lea, MN, 1953
- AA Degree, Bethel College, St. Paul, MN, 1955
- BS Degree, (Highest Distinction) Univ. of MN, 1957
- MA Degree, Western Michigan University, Kalamazoo, MI, 1960
- Education Doctorate, University of Illinois, Champaign/Urbana, IL, 1966

PROFESSIONAL SERVICE (Career Progression):
- <u>Teacher</u>: elementary; middle school, high school (5 years)
- <u>Elementary Principal</u>: pre-school; K-6 elementary, 1300 students (2 years)
- <u>Supervising Principal</u>: K-8, 3000 students (2 years)
- <u>High School Principal</u>: 9-12, 2000 students (4 years)
- <u>Adjunct Professor</u>: University of Illinois (summer session)
- <u>Assistant Superintendent for Instruction</u>: K-12 (2 years), Minnetonka School District
- <u>Superintendent</u>: K-12, (22 years), Minnetonka School District
- <u>Senior Fellow</u>; Lecturer of Record, Graduate School, Univ. of Minnesota
- <u>Keynote Speaker & Workshop Leader</u>: Search Institute of Minneapolis, (27 states, 250 assignments)
- <u>Consultant</u>: American Asset Management; Energy Education, Inc; Taher, Incorporated; Durrant Architects, Multiple MN School Districts
- <u>Author</u>: Nine Books

HONORS, AWARDS, RECOGNITIONS:
- USA Dept of Defense Sustained Superior Performance Award (top 1%) in Japan, 1963; Full Graduate School Tuition Scholarship,1964; Bush Foundation, Executive Fellows Award, 1981; MASA, Administrator of Excellence, 1987
- **President Suburban School Superintendents, USA, 1988**
- **MASA, MN Superintendent of the Year, 1990-91 (1 of 405)**
- **AASA, National Superintendent of the Year, 1990-91 (1 of 15,000)**
- Lake Conference Athletic Association Distinguished Service Award, 1992
- North Central Accreditation John W. Vaughn Excellence in Education Award, 1993
- Excelsior Chamber of Commerce, Person of the Year, 1995
- AASA Distinguished Service Award, 1998
- Co-Chair, AASA National Superintendent of the Year Selection Committee, 1997 to 2007
- Rotary District 5950 Ideals Award, 2007

Printed in the United States
By Bookmasters